PRINCE ANDREW

2.00

PRINCE ANDREW

Nicholas Courtney

Macdonald and Co
London & Sydney

A MACDONALD BOOK

© Nicholas Courtney 1983

This edition first published in Great Britain in 1983
by Macdonald & Co (Publishers) Ltd
London & Sydney

A BPCC Plc Company

ISBN 0 356 09962 8

This book was designed and produced by
The Rainbird Publishing Group Limited
40 Park Street
London W1Y 4DE

Typesetting by Electronic Village, London
Originated by Bridge Graphics Ltd, Hull
Printed in Great Britain by Jarrold Ltd, Norwich

Macdonald & Co (Publishers) Ltd
Maxwell House
74 Worship Street
London EC2A 2EN

ILLUSTRATION ACKNOWLEDGMENTS

Title page : Camera Press (Photo: Phil Rudge); Page 6 : Daily Telegraph Colour Library (Photo: Ken Mason); Page 7 (above) : Anwar Hussein; (below left) : Camera Press (Photo: Jim Bennett); (below right) : Camera Press (Photo: Jim Bennett); Page 8 : Camera Press (Photo: Jim Bennett); Page 9 (above) : Syndication International; (below) : Anwar Hussein; Page 10 : John Topham Picture Library; Page 11 : John Topham Picture Library; Page 13 : Popperfoto; Page 14 (left) : John Topham Picture Library; (right) : Camera Press (Photo: Studio Lisa); Page 15 (above) : Camera Press (Photo: John Scott); (below) : Camera Press (Photo: John Scott); Page 16 (above) : Camera Press (Photo: Studio Lisa); (below) : John Topham Picture Library; Page 17 : Syndication International; Page 18 (left) : Popperfoto; (right) : John Topham Picture Library; Page 19 : Syndication International; Page 20 : Camera Press (Photo: John Scott); Page 21 : Popperfoto; Page 22 : Camera Press (Photo: John Williams); Page 23 : Popperfoto; Page 24 : Camera Press (Photo: Mike Charity); Page 25 (both) : Syndication International; Page 26 (above) : Camera Press (Photo: Jon Blau); (below) : Camera Press (Photo: Norman Parkinson); Page 28 : Anwar Hussein; Page 29 : Syndication International; Page 30 : Anwar Hussein; Page 31 (both) : Anwar Hussein; Page 32 : Camera Press; Page 33 : Anwar Hussein; Page 34 : Syndication International; Page 35 : Anwar Hussein; Page 36 (both) : Syndication International; Page 37 : Anwar Hussein; Page 38 : Anwar Hussein; Page 39 (both) : Camera Press (Photo: John Scott); Page 40 : Anwar Hussein; Page 41 : Keystone; Page 42 : Anwar Hussein; Page 43 (above) : Syndication International; (below) : Anwar Hussein; Page 44 (both) : Anwar Hussein; Page 45 (above) : Camera Press (Photo: John Scott); (below) : Tim Graham; Page 47 (above) : Tim Graham; (below) : John Topham Picture Library; Page 48 (left) : Tim Graham; (right) : Anwar Hussein; Page 49 : John Topham Picture Library; Page 50 (above) : Syndication International; (below) : Anwar Hussein; Page 51 : Anwar Hussein; Page 52 : Syndication International; Page 53 (both) : Anwar Hussein; Page 54 (both) : Anwar Hussein; Page 55 : John Topham Picture Library; Page 57 (above) : Camera Press (Photo: Leonard Bourne); (below) : Camera Press (Photo: Bryn Colton); Page 58 : Popperfoto; Page 59 (left) : John Topham Picture Library; (right) : Express Newspapers; Page 60 : Duncan Paul Associates (Photo: Brian Aris); Page 61 : John Topham Picture Library; Page 62 (both) : Syndication International; Page 63 : Kim Sayer (both); Page 64 : Gerd Treuhaft.

CONTENTS

HERO'S RETURN

The sun finally broke through the Channel mist as the Royal Barge sped towards HMS *Invincible,* anchored off Spithead after her epic service in the Falklands Campaign. The Queen's Standard fluttered at the tiny masthead, for she, and the Duke of Edinburgh with Princess Anne, were aboard on their way to welcome home the aircraft carrier and the ship's company that included one very special helicopter pilot, their second son Sublieutenant HRH The Prince Andrew.

That day, 17 September 1982, began early on HMS *Invincible* with reveille played by a bugler at 5 o'clock. Shortly after 10 o'clock the Royal Barge came alongside and the Royal party came aboard. The formal ceremonies over, the Queen, the Duke of Edinburgh and Princess Anne went below for their private, family reunion with Prince Andrew in the Admiral's cabin. For twenty minutes they caught up on the news of the 166 days on active service, before they all appeared for photographers on their way to the bridge.

It was a highly charged scene as HMS *Invincible* inched her way into Portsmouth Harbour. Thousands had turned out to welcome her home, their deafening roar in competition with the blasts of ships' sirens and factory hooters. Red, white and blue balloons floated up into the cloudless sky, high above the cascades and spray of water from tugs' canon. Hundreds of ships, small boats, a paddle steamer and hovercraft all came out to escort her in. As she approached the West Wall of the harbour, a three-gun salute boomed over that cacophony. Then, at 12.40, the Captain gave the order 'Finish main engines' and HMS *Invincible* and her crew were home.

The Royal party came ashore with Prince Andrew. At the foot of the gangway a schoolgirl presented him with a red rose, supplied by a patriotic London florist, saying 'for your lady'. To the delight of the crowd, he clenched it between his teeth, then spun round to face his ship. With his cap high in the air, he leapt up and waved in jubilation to his brother officers and crewmen waiting to come ashore for their leave. It was a spontaneous action, one that typified the thrill, the relief and the emotional exhaustion of the whole ship's

Sublieutenant His Royal Highness the Prince Andrew with fellow officers of 820 Squadron on board HMS Invincible *on her triumphal return to England after the cessation of hostilities in the South Atlantic.*

Above: A family reunion on board HMS Invincible after Prince Andrew had been away on active service for nearly six months.
Below and right: Prince Andrew with the red rose presented to him by a schoolgirl. Red roses were given by a London florist to all the ship's company as they came ashore. The Queen and Princess Anne were presented with small baskets of red roses to match the single rose given to each man.

The Duke of Edinburgh in the uniform of Admiral of the Fleet with Prince Andrew. A former naval officer who saw active service during the Second World War, Prince Philip well understands the elation of a safe homecoming and a successful operation. Prince Andrew continues a strong naval tradition in the Royal Family and his Mountbatten great-grandfather, Prince Louis was First Sea Lord in the First World War.

company. The Queen was patently proud of every member of that Task Force and especially her son. They drove away to the cheers of the crowd, and for Prince Andrew, the first night away from his ship for nearly six months.

Earlier that morning, Prince Andrew had spoken to reporters. He told them that he had found the whole Campaign a tremendous experience and was proud to be a member of 820 Squadron. However, he admitted that, 'I [Prince Andrew] am not looking forward to going back to being a prince. I would gladly keep going – particularly with this ship's company and the men I have served with down in the Falklands.

'I am obviously looking forward to going home, but what awaits me when I get home – who knows? I think I have probably changed somewhat having seen what I have seen and felt what I have felt. I think my life has gone round a corner since I left five and a half months ago. I have to pick up where I left off. I have learned things about myself that I never would have learned anywhere else. I will wind down and re-acclimatize to life in the UK, the smell of the grass and the silence.'

Right: The spontaneous reaction of a jubilant Prince Andrew as he steps ashore.
Below: Of the thousands who came to see HMS Invincible _arrive home a few were additionally rewarded with the chance of talking to Prince Andrew before he drove off with his parents and sister to spend a few quiet days with his family._

1

THE YOUNG PRINCE

A crowd of around six hundred people waited all night outside Buckingham Palace in the freezing February air. Many others returned the next morning, hoping to be first with the news of the birth of the Queen's third child. Inside the Palace, the Queen had spent a comfortable night and the team of Royal physicians and midwife returned early in the morning. Still they all waited, and, at half-past three in the afternoon of 19 February 1960, Prince Andrew was born. Outside, a cheer went up as a Palace official posted the notice on the railings at 4.03 pm:

> 'The Queen was safely delivered of a son at 3.30 pm today. Her Majesty and the Infant Prince are both doing well.'

At that time, the Duke of Edinburgh was in his study waiting for the news. When Lord Evans, the Queen's physician, told him the good news, he bounded down the stairs with a bunch of white roses and carnations to the Queen and his new son.

The 'infant Prince' was born in the Belgium Suite and weighed 7 lb 3 oz. The Queen had decided on the ornate room with its large bathroom as it looked over the gardens behind the Palace. When she gave birth to her first child, Charles, twelve years before in the Buhl Room to the front of the Palace, the police had to quieten the huge crowd so that she could sleep. Two years later, her second child, Anne, was born at Clarence House.

Prince Philip had once said, 'People want their first child very much. They want the second almost as much. If a third comes along, they accept it as natural, but they haven't gone out of their way to try and get it.' So it was with the Queen and Prince Philip. They were married in 1947, and her father, George VI, although never strong, was reasonably expected to live for some considerable time. Sadly, he died in 1952, when her two children were still very young. She acceded to the throne and the immense responsibility as Sovereign shortly before her twenty-sixth birthday. Eight years

On a wintry February day in 1960 Fleet Street's evening newspapers carried the news of the birth of Prince Andrew a few hours earlier in the Belgium Suite at Buckingham Palace.

The first official photograph of the one-month-old Prince Andrew held by his sister, Princess Anne, then aged ten. This charming photograph was taken by Cecil Beaton, the leading royal photographer of his day.

later, with the inestimable help of Prince Philip, she had well mastered her position as Queen and felt able to cope with the months of pregnancy without it affecting her duties as monarch.

At the end of November the preceding year, a rather coy announcement appeared in the Court Circular that, from that date, the Queen would not be undertaking any further public engagements – Buckingham Palace parlance that the Queen was expecting another baby. She was, in fact, two months pregnant when she left for an exhaustive tour of Canada. Despite her doctors' advice to the contrary, the Queen was adamant that the tour should go ahead and only took the precaution of taking an extra seamstress with her to let out her clothes. Only one engagement, to Yellowknife in the North West Territories, was visited by Prince Philip alone. The Queen returned to England tired and exhausted after her great ordeal. Her doctors ordered her to rest and relax and, after a few days in bed, she retired to the bracing Scottish air of Balmoral for the remainder of the summer. For the rest of her pregnancy, the Queen led a quiet life, although she never relaxed over her 'Boxes' - the papers relating to matters of State – nor her official audiences, and only the day before her baby was due did she move down to the Belgium Suite for her confinement.

The usual excitement followed the birth. The crowds swelled in the Mall outside Buckingham Palace, and messages of congratulation flooded in from all over Britain, the Commonwealth and the rest of the world. The customary loyal message from the House of Commons was delivered by the Prime

Minister, Harold Macmillan; prayers were said, twenty-one gun salutes thundered out from Hyde Park and the Tower of London, flags topped buildings and, in almost a prophetic tribute to a future aviator, there was a flypast of the Black Arrows, a flying team made up of thirty-six Hunter jets, over the Palace. They were fitting tributes to a much-loved Queen and the first child born to a reigning monarch since the birth of Princess Beatrice to Queen Victoria in 1857.

The 'infant Prince' was christened Andrew Albert Christian Edward in the white and gold Music Room of Buckingham Palace by the Archbishop of Canterbury, Dr Fisher. This rich nomenclature was drawn from both sides of his family with historical overtures, two grandparents and two great-grandparents. He was christened Andrew after Prince Philip's father, Prince Andrew of Greece, and St Andrew of Scotland; Albert after the Queen's father (affectionately known as Bertie, although he adopted the name of George on his accession as king) and Queen Victoria's Consort, another Prince Albert, in deference to the Queen's wishes that all her descendants should bear the name of her beloved husband. Christian and Edward were the names of the great-grandparents – Christian IX of Denmark (the 'grandfather of Europe') and Edward VII, also the name of eight previous kings of varying age and distinction. It was a traditional Royal christening, with Andrew dressed in the Honiton lace robes, first made for the eldest son of Queen Victoria, the said Edward and the silver-gilt 'lily font' with water from the River Jordan. The sponsors, Royal godparents, came from the family and close friends – the Queen's uncle, the Duke of Gloucester, her cousins Princess Alexandra and the Master of Elphinstone, and two valued friends, the present Duke of Grafton and Mrs Harold Philips.

In addition to the christening, there was a change in the Royal surname. In recognition of the invaluable service of the Duke of Edinburgh as Consort, and of course as head of his family, the Queen joined his name with hers so that the Royal House should thereafter be known as Mountbatten-Windsor. She decreed that 'while I and my children shall continue to be styled and known as the House and family of Windsor, my descendants shall bear the name of Mountbatten-Windsor'.

From the moment of his birth, Andrew's upbringing was very different from his brother and sister, Charles and Anne. In their early years, the young Princess Elizabeth and later the Queen and her husband indulged the public's clamour for news and sight of their children. As a result, they became cult figures and considered 'public property'. Also, the new Queen was still feeling her way in her role as Sovereign, which robbed her of much of her enjoyment of her young children as a mother. With Andrew, the Queen and Prince Philip were determined that they should not be robbed a second time as parents. With that gap of nearly ten years, she had well mastered the complexities of her job and therefore had the confidence and experience to divide her time between the affairs of State and her family. The same was true of Prince Philip, who had carved himself out a role as Consort, second to the Queen, but very much as head of his family.

The policy began immediately. There were the official photographs of Andrew, taken by Cecil Beaton, shortly after he was born; then 'the wall of silence' went up around Buckingham Palace and nothing was seen or heard of him outside for months. Within the Palace, and at Windsor Castle at the weekends, a regular nursery routine developed. Gone was the stiff and starchy rule of Nanny Lightbody, who cared for Charles and Anne. Instead, Andrew's nursery was presided over by the former under-nanny, Mabel Anderson. The benign 'Mamba', as she was called by Andrew, can only have been amazed when her advertisement in the 'Situations Wanted' column of a nursing magazine was answered by the Comptroller of Clarence House – the then home of Princess Elizabeth, who was expecting Anne, and the Duke of Edinburgh. The daughter of a Liverpool policeman, she was a wholly capable nanny who combined exactly the right blend of firmness with affection to the maximum effect with her charges. With Mabel Anderson mainly responsible for Andrew, an under-nanny, June Waller, was engaged to look after Anne. Andrew had come just in time for Nanny Anderson, for, with Charles away at his preparatory school, Cheam, and Anne then nearly ten years old, her services were no longer really necessary. She did in fact stay for many years with the Royal Family, looking after Edward and then Princess Anne's first child, Peter Phillips.

The day and two night nurseries at Buckingham Palace are on the second floor in the north-west wing, just diagonally above the Queen's own apartments. With the more liberal regime of Nanny Anderson, Andrew would be given his breakfast in the nursery, then taken down to be with his parents in their rooms after they had dressed and breakfasted. The Royal Family have always been addicted to fresh air, and, whatever the weather, Andrew was placed in his pram in the garden or a corner of a courtyard with its ample hood up if it was raining. Occasionally, a passing policeman would notice that he was crying and his nanny would be summoned.

The Queen especially enjoyed 'Mabel's night off', when she could bath Andrew herself and put him to bed. Whenever possible, she had always kept bathtime free for her children, even going to the extent of asking her then Prime Minister, Winston Churchill, to delay their regular meeting by an hour, so that she could be with Charles and Anne. Weekends were usually spent at Windsor, and Nanny Anderson would take Andrew and Anne down after lunch on Fridays. There, the Queen and Prince Philip could see more of him than in London and, in a way, he brought back to his parents a renewed sense of youth and fun.

Even the most ardent of the 'Royal' reporters and photographers failed to glean anything of the new baby. The more direct and irresponsible of the continental press went as far as to suggest that there was something seriously wrong with Andrew, which was why he was never seen in public or photographed. Their prognosis was dispelled when, as an afterthought, he was included in the official photographs of Queen Elizabeth the Queen Mother to mark her sixtieth birthday. The photographs showed a particularly 'jolly' baby, 'always full of smiles', and 'who rarely cried'. To those who knew Prince Philip when he was that age, Andrew looked exactly like his father, with his ash-blond hair and deep blue eyes. No word of him or photograph appeared for a further ten months, until the Queen's official birthday in June 1961. A huge crowd had gathered before Buckingham Palace for the traditional balcony appearance of the Queen and members of her family. That year, they had an added thrill, for, on the stroke of one o'clock, the Queen appeared in her scarlet uniform holding the young Andrew in her arms. The great cheering was momentarily drowned by the roar of a squadron of sixteen Javelin fighters as they passed overhead in Royal salute.

Up to the time that Andrew went off to join his ship in the Royal Navy, he had always followed the Royal 'migration'. The week was spent at Buckingham Palace, the weekends at Windsor Castle. Christmas was spent at Sandringham in Norfolk, the Queen's private estate, until the Royal Family grew so large with wives and children that the house was not large enough to accommodate them all, so the vast Windsor Castle was used instead. New Year, however, is always spent at Sandringham and the Royal Family stays there until the end of January. The summer holidays traditionally begin in August, when Prince Philip is host to a party aboard the Royal Yacht *Britannia* for Cowes Week, the famous yachting event off the Isle of Wight. The rest of the summer is spent at Balmoral, the Queen's estate in the north of Scotland, and then at the beginning of October, they 'go back to work'.

It was in this rarefied life of privilege that Andrew grew up, but, to the credit of his parents, he was not spoilt. Prince Philip maintained that however hard they tried to bring up their offspring 'as ordinary children' it was a virtually impossible task. From birth, they live in palaces and castles with endless servants and organized by a Household who bow to their parents. Their mother's features are on stamps and coins, and crowds gather to cheer wherever they go. That they are as unspoilt as they are is due to Prince Philip, who, with his drive, enthusiasm and dominance, is very much the head of his family and an example to his children. He has always been a caring father, encouraging them wherever they showed promise or interest. If he was strict or harsh on them, it was because he knew that any lapse of effort or drop in standards would rebound on them later and cause a deeper problem.

Within that world of privilege and parental care, Andrew grew up to be a robust and sturdy little boy. He was also an engaging child and a great favourite of both his grandmothers. Queen Elizabeth the Queen Mother admitted that 'half the fun of being a grandmother is being able to spoil your grandchildren', and Andrew was no exception. Likewise his paternal grandmother,

A happy photograph taken in the garden at Clarence House in London to mark the Queen Mother's sixtieth birthday in August 1960 showed her holding her latest grandson, Prince Andrew, who was then nearly six months old.

Princess Andrew of Greece, who lived at Buckingham Palace. Andrew's mannerisms reminded her of her son, who would hunch his shoulders about his ears when anything excited or perplexed him. When Andrew was a little older, he was allowed to play in the Queen's study while she was busy with her 'Boxes', and those who had regular audiences with her soon became used to the little boy, quietly engaged with some puzzle or looking at a picture book in the corner of the room. Such a departure would have been unthinkable with Charles and Anne as her study was strictly out of bounds. With Andrew, the Queen found it an added opportunity to be with her youngest son. She also found time to teach him the alphabet, count and tell the time on a large clock face. Outside, it was the Queen who started him off on his first pony, a minute Shetland pony called Mr Dinkum. She would hold Andrew in the saddle as she had done with such

The two and a half-year-old Prince Andrew with his nanny, Miss Mabel Anderson, the daughter of a Liverpool policeman, and Princess Anne arriving at Kings Cross Station on their way back from a holiday at Balmoral.

The young prince in the nursery at Buckingham Palace. Whenever the Queen and Prince Philip were away on overseas tours, Prince Andrew was well looked after by his two grandmothers with whom he was a great favourite.

effect with her older children, who, in particular Anne, had gone on to become very proficient riders. Prince Philip also played his part. Known to all his children as 'Papa', he took Andrew in hand, teaching him to swim in the Palace swimming pool and playing games of football inside the nursery and in the extensive grounds of Windsor and Buckingham Palace.

Just as they had been separated for Andrew's first birthday when the Queen and Prince Philip visited India, Pakistan and Nepal, so they missed his third birthday with their tour of Australia and New Zealand. Of course he missed his parents, but he always had both his grandmothers to spoil him when they were away. As far as Andrew was concerned, Charles had always been away at school during termtime, first at Cheam, then at Gordonstoun in Scotland but, in the autumn of 1963, Anne too went away to a boarding school, Benenden in Kent. Although Anne played with him after her own lessons, he was so much younger than her and her departure did not affect him that much. Anyway, both Charles and Anne were there in the school holidays. Andrew was left in the nursery to enjoy the undivided attention of his nanny, his parents and grandparents. He was not to enjoy their sole attention for long. Shortly after his fourth birthday, the Queen and Prince Philip's fourth child, Edward, was born on 10 March 1964. Their family was now com-

plete, with a spread in ages of over fifteen years. Edward's birth also coincided neatly with the Royal 'baby boom' of cousins. Only five years separate Andrew and his cousin Marina Ogilvy, and barely three months separate Edward, Sarah (daughter of Princess Margaret and Lord Snowdon), James Ogilvy (son of the Hon Angus Ogilvy and Princess Alexandra) and Helen (daughter of the Duke and Duchess of Kent). This younger set of cousins included George (Earl of St Andrews, Helen's elder brother) and David (Viscount Linley, Sarah's elder brother), both just younger than Andrew. They began as close friends and have remained so, despite their different life-styles.

In those early years, Andrew was a popular little boy with the Palace staff. At the Queen's insistence, they called him plain Andrew, while he, with instilled politeness, addressed them by their surname and their relevant title. 'Below stairs' he was, however, known as Andy Pandy after the then popular puppet on children's television. That relationship was not to last. He had an obstinate streak if he did not have his own way which made life difficult for the Palace staff, but he also possessed disarming, 'little-boy' charm. Most admired his zest for life and, as his paternal aunts commented, he was like his father 'sometimes naughty, never nasty'. Usually, he made his presence felt with shouts of laughter, cries of anguish or an unbridled

Top: The Queen and Prince Andrew watching an event at the Braemer Highland Gathering not far from Balmoral. These highland games have taken place in September every year since 1832.
Above: On the balcony of Buckingham Palace, Lord Mountbatten points out to his great nephew, Prince Andrew and his cousin, Viscount Linley, the traditional RAF flypast which takes place after Trooping the Colour.

curiosity for whatever was happening at the time. Traditionally, the Royal Family have always been keen on practical jokes and Andrew was no exception. One unsuspecting footman was laying the table for lunch when the knives and forks disappeared as soon as his back was turned. Andrew, the culprit, was discovered amid peals of laughter behind a chair, clutching the missing knives and forks.

Even at that young age, Andrew idolized his father,

15

Above: A photograph taken to mark Prince Andrew's sixth birthday shows him with his younger brother, Prince Edward in the grounds of Buckingham Palace. In the early days, official birthday photographs were all that were seen of the young princes.
Right: Six-year-old Prince Andrew pictured here wearing a Wild West fringed suede jacket when he accompanied the Queen to Windsor Great Park one Sunday to watch his father, one of the top English players, play polo.

a respect that is as strong today as then. In return, Prince Philip has always enjoyed Andrew's company, relishing his extrovert nature and boisterous behaviour. He was tough too, with his full share of childish accidents. He twice fell into the fountain in the garden of Windsor Castle, seemingly with no ill effects. On another occasion, he earned his title of 'that young imp' given to him by the Palace staff when he removed the back of Nanny Anderson's wireless and took out the valves.

Those carefree days of the nursery, the learning 'at his mother's knee' and the boisterous romping with his father all too soon were drawing to a close for Andrew when he reached the age of five. It was decided that he should follow his brother and sister into the school-room at Buckingham Palace and start his lessons 'for real'.

2

GROWING UP

Once again, Andrew benefited from the lessons learned by his parents in the bringing up of his elder brother, Charles, and sister, Anne. Both had been taught in the school-room at Buckingham Palace by Miss Katherine Peebles, who had previously taught the Duchess of Kent's two younger children, Alexandra and Michael. Miss Peebles, or 'Mispy' as she was affectionately called, was middle-aged, diminutive and very alert. She had no formal training but, with her calm temperament, she was ideally suited to teaching the nervous, somewhat touchy, Charles. He remained in a 'class of one', competition being thought bad for him. When Anne moved into the school-room, she shared her lessons with two other girls of her own age.

Mispy was recalled to teach Andrew and four contemporaries. They were all drawn from the children of friends or members of the Household. Katie Seymour is the daughter of Major Raymond Seymour, an extra equerry to Queen Elizabeth the Queen Mother and a director of the brewery firm Whitbread and Company; the other girl was the Honourable Victoria Butler, daughter of Lord Dunboyne, a circuit court judge. The two boys were Jamie Steel and Justin Beaumont whose grandfather, Lord Allendale had been an equerry to Andrew's grandfather, George VI. The quartet was joined later by David Linley.

The school-room was really a sitting room situated above the Balcony Room in the front of the Palace. Smart wooden desks replaced the green baize card tables of Anne's day and hard pine chairs the Regency striped chairs from the corridor. The rest of the room was simply furnished with a large desk for Miss Peebles, a wall map of the world, a globe, a blackboard and an easel. Mispy's pupils were taught the three 'R's', reading, writing and arithmetic, as well as geography, history and scripture. Later French was added to the curriculum. Outside the school-room, Andrew and his fellow pupils went to dancing classes with Madame Vacani and later he began rudimentary lessons on the piano. By way of exercise, the boys played football and cricket and ran at the Brigade of Guards' Cricket Club at Burton Court, opposite the Royal Hospital in Chelsea, not that far from the Palace. They were also put through their paces in the Chelsea Barracks gymnasium by one of the staff sergeants. Where Charles was recognized and photographed at every turn, the

The first official engagement of Prince Andrew, wearing the wolf cub uniform as he takes the salute during a march past of a thousand Queen's scouts at the St George's Day parade at Windsor Castle in 1968.

young Andrew could move about London totally unrecognized.

Mispy was well able to control the natural exuberance of Andrew and channel it into more worthwhile pursuits. She was happy to report to his parents that he showed great flair and aptitude once he had mastered the need for discipline. However, his fellow pupils did not always see eye to eye with him, for he was prone to throwing his weight about. He could be aggressive when in a black mood, which frequently upset his classmates, but it was not long before they had the measure of him and gave as good as he delivered. To their credit, they all remained friends after their paths diverged, particularly Katie Seymour, whose parents often invited Andrew to stay at their house at Bembridge on the Isle of Wight.

In order to meet other girls of their own age, the Queen, as Princess Elizabeth, was enrolled as a Girl Guide. Both she and her sister, Princess Margaret, enjoyed their meetings enormously and consequently a Brownie troop, the 'Ist B/ham Palace Troop', was formed. Yet again, Andrew benefited from the successful experiments of his elder brother and sister and joined a Wolf Cub pack – the Ist Marylebone, where he learned to mix with others. Andrew loved it all and greatly enjoyed the experience of meeting other boys of the same age and from other walks of life. His fellow Cubs were a cosmopolitan lot – among them, the young sons of an upholsterer, a Pakistani immigrant shopkeeper, a bank caretaker and an Inspector in the Police. Possibly it would have been better if he could have gone to a draughty church hall, where most Scout and Cub packs meet, but the Queen and Prince Philip were both anxious that Andrew should not attract any undue publicity, so spoiling his enjoyment of the event. Instead, the Cubs met in the grounds of Buckingham Palace, arriving for their weekly meetings in a mini-bus.

Another outside activity for Andrew was learning to skate. Once a week, for eight weeks, he was taken to Wimbledon Ice Rink for a half-hour lesson with the coach, Roy Lee. Lee was nervous of teaching his pupil and terrified that he might 'break his skull'. His fears were unfounded and Andrew managed to skate with a degree of skill. Other coaching came from Dan Maskell, the former Wimbledon tennis champion, who had also coached Anne, and Len Muncer, the great Glamorgan cricketer, who put him through his paces at the Lords Cricket Ground.

For his sixth birthday, Andrew was given a very special present by his parents, a miniature Aston Martin presented to them during their visit to the car works. It was an exact, scaled-down replica of the one used in the James Bond film Goldfinger. Dark blue in colour with the personalized number of JBOO7, it had artificial machine guns concealed in the sidelights and a smoke-screen system. He was exceptionally lucky that birthday too, as he received a pony called Willy, a seven-year-old grey. Andrew was thrilled with his presents, even though there were now hours of riding instruction from the Crown Equerry, Lt-Col., now Sir, John Miller.

The Queen and six-year-old Prince Andrew leaving Westminster Abbey after the wedding of the then Marquis of Hamilton to Miss Sacha Phillips where Prince Andrew was one of the pages.

An enthusiastic wolf cub, Prince Andrew was a member of the 1st Marylebone Pack for six months before he went off to prep school. He so enjoyed the meetings that a special cub pack was started there.

But such presents are well beyond the reach of most children, and as he grew older, Andrew became increasingly aware of the chasm between him and others. It would therefore be natural for Andrew to think he was someone special. The problem did not arise with Charles, who was painfully shy and had absolutely no illusions of grandeur. Anne had far more self-confidence. With the assertiveness of a second child, Anne channelled her energies into succeeding at her chosen pastimes, such as her ponies, where she triumphed. But with Andrew it was different. He was, and is, extrovert and outgoing. As the Queen once commented, 'Andrew isn't a bit shy.' That, coupled with his rich and privileged background, appeared to some as arrogance. However, his father saw to it that the trait was channelled into more agreeable qualities in the child, and it was with some pride that he was heard to remark that his son 'was a natural boss'.

The Royal Family have always enjoyed practical jokes. Andrew's great-grandparents, Edward VII and Queen Alexandra, as Prince and Princess of Wales, were experts in the making of apple-pie beds and deadly accurate with soda-syphons after dinner. Once, the Prince put a dead seagull in the bed of a friend who had had too much to drink. As a boy of six, Prince Philip, aided by his cousin, Princess Alexandra of Greece, opened the door of a pigsty on the home farm at Panka, the summer house on the Baltic of his aged aunt Sophie. Philip chased the pigs out but could not stop them before they overran a tea-party on the lawns. Charles, too, enjoys a practical joke and has substituted custard pies for the soda syphons of his great-grandparents. Once, as a boy, he pressed a well-sucked boiled sweet into his mother's gloved hand just before she left the Royal car to meet some dignitary. With this great 'tradition' behind him, it is not surprising that Andrew turned out to be a great practical joker as well.

Where the Queen, then the young Princess Elizabeth, and Charles would go out of their way not to pass a sentry, thus earning a 'present arms', Princess Margaret and Anne, as girls, would deliberately walk up and down in front of them to hear the clatter of their rifles and the stamp of their boots as they presented arms. Andrew was more subtle. He derived considerable satisfaction from tying their bootlaces together as they stood motionless on duty, not permitted to move. An irate sergeant then had to go round freeing the Royal guard.

The Palace servants also came in for Andrew's pranks. Housemaids would answer bells to seemingly empty rooms only to find a small boy hiding behind a sofa. An inquiry was mounted· when a particularly large and valuable silver tray went missing. The culprit, Andrew, was soon caught, using it as a toboggan for sliding down the wide stairs of Buckingham Palace.

Guests, too, came in for his particular brand of humour. At one of the garden parties at Buckingham Palace, no one was quite sure whether it was he who turned the signs round, directing the guests all over the garden and the Palace in total chaos. Even with his family, his practical joking wore a little thin. Once, they had all decided to swim in the pool at Windsor

At the Royal Windsor Horse Show in 1967, Prince Andrew presented the Queen's Challenge Cup to the winning team, watched by Lt-Col. John Miller, the Queen's Equerry.

Castle. When they arrived, the water was covered with a thick layer of bubbles. Someone had poured a whole bottle of bubble-bath liquid into the inlet so that it foamed up all over the warm water. That day, swimming was cancelled. No one knew who did it and no one owned up, but the finger of suspicion obviously pointed to Andrew. Where most who met Andrew thought him a 'sturdy, lively youngster, energetic and full of beans', it was not the view of all – particularly those on the butt of his practical jokes. The Queen once conceded that 'he is not always a little ray of sunshine about the house'.

Andrew's pre-school life fell into a predictable routine of the 'Royal migration'; London, Windsor, Sandringham and Balmoral, with the occasional visit to the Royal Yacht _Britannia_. To him, and his brothers and sister, this meant a very close family life. He looked forward to the post-Christmas gathering of his family at Sandringham, with the excitement of his cousins and the shoots and the chance to walk with the beaters. He loved watching the Queen handle her gun

Prince Andrew is fortunate in having many cousins of his own age. It was an annual treat every Easter holidays to stay with the Duke of Beaufort at Badminton. (From left to right) Lady Helen Windsor, Lady Sarah Armstrong-Jones, the Earl of St Andrews, Viscount Linley and Prince Andrew.

dogs, black labradors, as they retrieved the shot pheasants. There were children's parties of various Norfolk neighbours to go to – not least the younger children of Viscount and Viscountess Althorp, Diana and Charles, who lived at Park House, within the grounds of Sandringham. Years later, their daughter was known worldwide as Lady Diana Spencer, now the Princess of Wales. Often it snowed and there were snowball fights on the terrace with his brothers and sister. Andrew, being a plucky little boy, was always in the thickest part of any such fight. Sometimes the lakes and duck-flighting ponds froze over and Andrew, with the rest of his family, would skate, showing off what he had learned at the Wimbledon Ice Rink. He rode his pony Willy, which was boxed along with the other riding horses belonging to the Royal Family to wherever they were in residence.

The real Royal Family holiday begins in August at Balmoral. There was always intense excitement when the Royal Family packed up and left on the Royal Train for Ballater, the local station to the Castle. Andrew, already with his daily tasks of feeding, watering and grooming his own corgi, was also responsible for her on the journey. The comfortable train with sleeping compartments, bathrooms, dining-room and large sitting-room, travelled overnight and, the next morning, they would arrive ready for their holidays. Balmoral has been a favourite Royal residence since it

was bought by Queen Victoria and rebuilt by her husband, Prince Albert. Every generation since, the Royal Family have 'gone native'. They wear kilts, tartan and tweed. Andrew indignantly refused to wear 'trews' under his kilt as he knew none of the men wore them.

There was always plenty to do at Balmoral. Prince Philip taught Andrew the rudiments of sailing in the catamaran he kept on Loch Muick, a large expanse of inland water on the Balmoral Estate. There, the Queen could relax completely, almost free from the affairs of State, and spend more time with her family. There were long walks and picnics, and barbecues at the Old School House on the shores of Loch Muick. When it rained, which it frequently did, there were games of Scrabble and another Royal pastime, jigsaw puzzles; the Queen always has a large and difficult one 'on the go' and, through many years of experience, is an expert. Also, there were the visits to Craithie Church for Matins every Sunday and the excitement of the Highland Gathering at Braemar. For Andrew, they were enchanted days. He loved, and still loves, the place and the people. There have always been busy, fun house-parties of all ages, friends and Household of his parents and Queen Elizabeth the Queen Mother, younger friends of Charles and Anne, as well as the officers of the regiment on guard duty. He had his cousins, Princess Margaret's children, David and Sarah, as well as the Ogilvy and Kent children, to play with, although there were frequent cousinly squabbles between them. They were happy holidays and the return to the rigours of their life at the end of the summer was always a little sad. After the summer of 1968, when Andrew was eight and a half, he had more than the school-room and his nursery life to look forward to, as it had been decided to send him away to a boarding preparatory school.

3

SCHOOL DAYS

A new era began for Andrew when he was sent to Heatherdown, an exclusive preparatory school near Ascot, chosen by the Queen and Prince Philip for its nearness to Windsor rather than for its caché as one of the preparatory schools for Eton. Andrew went straight from the school-room to his boarding school. With his extrovert character, there was no need for a 'breaking-in' period as for his brother, Charles. Charles spent two terms at Hill House, a day school in London, to accustom him to be with other boys of his own age before going onto his father's school of Cheam. The venture was very nearly a failure, as the press and crowds swamped him so much on his first day that the

Prince Andrew aged eight and a half, arriving at Heatherdown for his first day at school accompanied by Prince Philip. The only concession at school made to his royal status was the presence of his detective.

Queen thought of abandoning the scheme altogether. When he went to Cheam, Prince Charles was a shy, lonely and miserable little boy.

Andrew was very different. For a start, he was a different character and physically tougher. With the precedent set that the Queen's children should go away to school, it was no surprise that Andrew should follow suit. As the younger son, he did not command the same 'press' as his older brother, the future Prince of Wales and first in line to the throne.

Heatherdown suited Andrew well. It was a gaunt, Victorian red-brick building set in thirty acres of formal and rough gardens, with football, cricket and rugby pitches. There was also a swimming-pool. The headmaster, James Edwards, made sure that his Royal pupil was treated in exactly the same way as every other pupil in the school. 'The object', he explained, 'is to let him lead as normal a schoolboy life as possible.' His policy towards Andrew worked well and he was followed by George, Earl of St Andrews, eldest son of the Duke and Duchess of Kent, and later by Andrew's younger brother Edward.

This sameness began with his school uniform. He arrived with the Queen wearing a grey flannel suit with short trousers with the distinctive red school tie and cap. He was allowed the same pocket money as the other boys and the same number of 'exeats' – weekends at home. Like all new boys, he shared a dormitory with six other boys. The only concession made to his Royal status was the presence of his detective. Andrew, like his sister at Benenden, enjoyed the school immensely. His day began at a quarter-past seven. After breakfast there were lessons from 9 o'clock until 12.30 – a mixture of English, French, Latin, mathematics, physics and chemistry, biology, history, scripture and geography as well as music and carpentry. The afternoons were for sport, soccer and rugby football in the winter terms, cricket, tennis, swimming and athletics in the summer term.

Despite being a new boy, the lowest of the low in any boarding school, Andrew certainly made his presence felt from the beginning, both with the staff and the boys. His confident manner and competitive streak were often read as arrogance. He was occasionally unco-operative with members of the staff and antagonistic towards his fellow pupils. However, the 'natural boss' came through and Andrew soon established himself as the leader of his group of friends. With his good grounding with Miss Peebles, he did tolerably well at his lessons. He returned for the Christmas holidays with that assured swagger of all prep-school boys after that first term away from home. He also felt that much more 'grown-up' as he, like Charles and Anne before him, had been away to school, not like his younger brother Edward, who was still in the school-room at home.

The spring holidays were fun in a different way as the television film *Royal Family* was being shot at various of the Royal Palaces. It was a great excitement for Andrew, who appeared briefly in a group scene. He came across as 'a lively, cheerful boy with a touch of the daredevil in his glance'.

During that summer term, Charles was invested as Prince of Wales on 1 July 1969. Andrew was not allowed to attend the ceremony, but, in common with millions of others, watched it on television. After the celebrations were over, the Queen organized a holiday on the Royal Yacht *Britannia* before retiring to Balmoral for the rest of the summer. Andrew joined the Royal party from Bembridge on the Isle of Wight, where he had been staying with his friend from school-room days, Katie Seymour. There, he sailed in small dinghies and played on the beach like any other small boy, unnoticed by the press or the public.

The Royal Yacht left Hull for the start of their cruise which began in the Shetland Isles. From there they sailed to Norway to visit their cousins King Olaf and Crown Prince Harald and his young wife, Princess Sonja. They met at Bergen and, accompanied by the Norwegian royal yacht, *Norge,* sailed north, exploring the beautiful coastline and fjords. The Queen does not care for sailing and Andrew was considered too young to join Prince Philip, the Prince of Wales and Princess Anne on his yacht *Bloodhound* for their extended cruise in Norwegian waters. He was bitterly disappointed, particularly as the yawl was to be sold for reasons of economy shortly after the cruise.

Throughout his five years at Heatherdown, Andrew's life was very much a predictable routine of working his way up the school and enjoying his

---

While at Sandringham during the Easter holidays of 1969, Prince Andrew became involved in the making of the BBC film, Royal Family, *the first of its kind ever to be made.*

holidays. In the Christmas term of 1970, he was joined by his cousin, George, the young Earl of St Andrews. He was a particularly bright boy and did well to win a scholarship to Eton at the end of his five years at Heatherdown. He was, however, better remembered for his arrival than for his scholarly departure. Scotland Yard had had a tip-off that there was an IRA plot to kidnap him from his school at the start of the Easter term for an exchange for imprisoned terrorists. The message was unclear and it was thought that Andrew could have been involved as well. At the start of the term, Heatherdown was besieged by Special Branch officers who mounted a twenty-four-hour watch on the school, in particular on Andrew and George. The staff found it difficult to keep the place running smoothly, but, not unnaturally, the boys found it a huge joke, except for the two Royal boys, who found police surveillance restricting.

Later that term, in March, Andrew was in a party from Heatherdown visiting the Natural History Museum in South Kensington, London. A fight broke out between three boys from the East End and the tail-enders of the Heatherdown group. Two of the boys from Heatherdown were hurt, not seriously, before the fight was stopped. Because Andrew was there, although not actively involved, it attracted more attention than it warranted.

During those Easter holidays, Andrew joined the traditional Royal party to Badminton, the seat of the Duke of Beaufort and venue of the three day event Horse Trials. That particular event in 1971 had even more meaning to Andrew, as his sister was competing in her first Badminton Horse Trial on the Queen's horse Doublet. After an exciting three days, Princess Anne came fifth overall, the event being won by Andrew's future brother-in-law, Mark Phillips, on Great Ovation. Her success was enough to qualify her for an individual place in the European Championship at Burghley, which, with immense family pride and sheer guts after an operation, Princess Anne won to become European Champion.

With the success of the cruise to Norway, the Queen decided to repeat the holiday, and the whole Royal Family went up to the very north of Scotland on the Royal Yacht *Britannia*. They anchored in the mouth of the Thurso River and visited the Castle of Mey, Queen Elizabeth the Queen Mother's romantic Scottish home between Thurso and John o' Groats.

The events of Andrew's life did not change much outside the regular pattern of school and the fun of the school holidays. His father taught him to shoot, although it was a long time before he was privileged to join any of the driven shoots at Sandringham or Balmoral. At Christmas, 1971 he appeared briefly in the Queen's Christmas Message, prerecorded but shown throughout Britain and the Commonwealth. Andrew appeared with his brother Edward, turning the pages of an old family photograph album while the Queen talked about their forebears. Also during those holidays, the Bishop of Norwich, the Right Reverend Maurice Wood, took Andrew to watch a football match, a home match between Norwich and Chelsea. Andrew greatly enjoyed the game but, contrary to

In August 1969 Prince Andrew enjoyed an informal seaside holiday at Bembridge on the Isle of Wight, staying with the family of one of his former schoolroom companions, Katie Seymour.

popular opinion, is not a football supporter. That academic year, both younger brothers were at Heatherdown together, Andrew at the top, Edward a new boy working his way up through the school. As the school was not that large, they invariably met, but Edward was keen to make his own way and not be under the shadow of his elder brother.

During that last year at Heatherdown, Andrew played rugby for the school First XV and also cricket for the First XI. Like his father, he showed promise as a cricketer and benefited from his coaching at Lords. With his early training and instruction from his father, he swam well. That last term at his prep school, he took and passed his Common Entrance examination.

Suddenly, he had grown up. Being mostly in the company of 'grown-ups', his family, their friends, Members of the Household and Palace servants, he was totally at ease in their company. At the age of thirteen, he began to be seen on State occasions, such as the Trooping the Colour, a fabulous parade

of the Brigade of Guards to mark the Sovereign's birthday. Andrew joined the procession, travelling with his grandmother, Queen Elizabeth the Queen Mother, in the State Landau. He enjoyed the experience enormously, it was so much better than watching on television as he had done in the past. He waved to the crowds and warmed to their cheers.

The staff at Heatherdown were not sorry to see Andrew leave, but they wished him luck when he left. With Heatherdown behind him and Common Entrance passed, he began his summer holidays. They began at Cowes, where he stayed on the Royal Yacht, and this time he was allowed to crew on _Yeoman XIX,_ the yacht his father had borrowed to compete in the Britannia Cup. Later he went up to Balmoral, where this time he fished the River Dee, was allowed to accompany a guest and a ghillie out stalking and to join the guns, as a spectator, for the grouse shooting. He did not return with the rest of the Royal Family at the end of the holidays. He had passed the necessary exams and been accepted by Gordonstoun and was to follow in the footsteps of his father and elder brother.

Andrew was only too well aware of what was expected of him at Gordonstoun. Both his father and elder brother had been 'Guardians' – the Gordonstoun equivalent of headboy, while his father had also been captain of cricket and hockey and a good athlete.

When he left, the headmaster wrote: 'Prince Philip is universally trusted, liked, and respected. He had the greatest sense of service of all the boys in the school. Prince Philip's leadership qualities are most noticeable, though marred at times by impatience and intolerance. He will need the exacting demand of a great service to do justice to himself. His best is outstanding; his second best is not good enough. Prince Philip will make his mark in any profession where he will have to prove himself in a full trial of strength.' On the other hand, the Prince of Wales had also excelled at the school. As an actor, he is best remembered for his sterling performance of Macbeth. Father and son had both set a high standard, a difficult one for Andrew to follow.

As it had been for Charles, Eton had been a possibility as a school for Andrew, but the same drawbacks remained. Eton was too open a school, its houses, classrooms and games fields being scattered all over the town, the Etonians' distinctive dress inviting hoards of tourists, press and photographers. That was precisely the kind of publicity the Queen and Prince Philip wished to avoid. It was also too close to Windsor and there would be the temptation to 'sneak' home. Gordonstoun, in a remote part of the Highlands of Scotland, was the only real choice of school for Andrew.

The school of Gordonstoun was founded in Scotland

Since 1949 the Duke of Beaufort has hosted the famous international three day event at Badminton. The Royal Family, including Prince Andrew from an early age, have been keen supporters.

by Dr Kurt Hahn in 1933. Hahn had earlier founded Salem, a school designed to bring out the best in its pupils by their own enterprise, elitism and sense of community spirit. One of the first pupils was Prince Berthold, who later married Prince Philip's sister, Princess Theodora of Greece. After Cheam, Prince Philip went to Salem, but, with the rise of Nazism in Germany, the Jewish Hahn had to flee with a handful of pupils. One of those pupils was Prince Philip, who later was responsible for some of the actual building work when the school took over the imposing stone country house of Gordonstoun, close to the Moray Firth in the north-east corner of Scotland. Like Salem, the school motto is *Plus est en vous* (There is more in you). It was, and of course still is, rigorously applied to all pupils. Hahn believed that self-reliance and self-confidence were the prime factors for a good citizen and that these could only be achieved through a high degree of fitness. Another way of promoting his pupils to their best was through community service, and they still man the the school's fire brigade, coastguard station and mountain and ocean rescue teams. Over the years, they have saved many lives.

The Gordonstoun that Andrew went to for the Michaelmas term of 1973 was very different to the one the Prince of Wales left six years before. The headmaster had changed. 'Just after Prince Charles left a new headmaster – myself – [John Kempe] came to the school with new ideas.' Where the spirit and ideals of the school remained the same, the austere and often forbidding bleakness of the place mellowed. The academic side also improved out of all recognition and Oxbridge entries became the norm rather than the rare exception. The headmaster was quick to point out that 'whatever the school's reputation was or is, it is not an extremely Spartan school. We have central heating and a swimming-pool heated to seventy-five degrees.' Cold showers after early morning runs were abandoned and sports, rugby football and cricket, were played more often, in line with other schools.

The greatest innovation of all was the introduction of girls into the school. When Andrew arrived, there were thirty girls and, during the five years he was at Gordonstoun, the number increased steadily.

Andrew arrived with his father and his second cousin, Amanda Knatchbull, who had been staying at Balmoral before the term started. After meeting the headmaster and some of the staff, Andrew's first term began. Like his father, but unlike his elder brother, Andrew loved his time at Gordonstoun. The toughness of the place and the abundance of physical activity suited his boisterous nature. The system was good for him too. When he left Heatherdown, he was at the top of the school in a position of relative importance. At Gordonstoun, he had to start back at the bottom. He found it demeaning to be in such a lowly position and resorted to boasting about his position and rank as younger son of the Queen. That, coupled with his natural competitive spirit and inherent self-confidence, made him deeply unpopular. One of his contemporaries recalled that first term later: 'There was a bit of "I am a Prince" about him when he first arrived. But you can't get away with that sort of thing at Gordonstoun and it was soon knocked out of him. The ribbings he got were unmerciful and he caught on fast. He had to.'

Above: The Royal Family spend much of the late summer each year on holiday at Balmoral with their friends, horses and dogs.

Right: Another highlight of the school holidays for the younger members of the Royal Family was a visit to the Royal Tournament at Earl's Court, London each July when the armed services put on a programme of exciting and colourful events. Here the Queen takes Prince Andrew, then fourteen years old, to visit the tournament.

Andrew soon knuckled down to the regime and lived exactly as every other boy. He had the same pocket money, then about £10 per term, and, although Balmoral was only sixty miles away, the same number of exeats. One departure from the norm was being allowed to attend his sister's wedding. Princess Anne married Captain Mark Phillips on 14 November 1973 – also Prince Charles's birthday. Andrew flew down in an Andover of the Queen's Flight in time for the actual wedding, but not for the reception and ball at Buckingham Palace beforehand. It was a glittering occasion in Westminster Abbey and once again Andrew travelled in the procession with Queen Elizabeth the Queen Mother. Edward,

was a page, with his cousin Sarah Armstrong-Jones as bridesmaid. Princess Anne just had two of them, dismissing more as 'yards of unwanted children'. Although he missed the ball, he did attend the wedding breakfast – really a lunch – held in the 'ball supper-room'. Later, a very happy and cheerful Royal Family made their balcony appearance to the delight of the crowd. Princess Anne and her new husband went off to the West Indies on the Royal Yacht for their honeymoon while Andrew returned to finish his first term at Gordonstoun.

By the end of that first term, Andrew had settled into his new school and, like Heatherdown, had established himself as the head of a small group of friends. After the initial spell of perversity, the staff found an eager and willing pupil with an inquiring mind. He was quicker than his brother and did not share his difficulty with mathematics or science subjects. On the games field, he showed promise as a tolerable cricketer and a strong swimmer. Although not by any means universally popular, Andrew was well thought of by at least one member of the staff. He declared 'He [Andrew] has no time for sychophants and if anyone tries to take the mickey out of him, he fights back. He's just as good with the verbalistics as with his fists.' At that time, only one story filtered out of the school and that was a minor incident which the headmaster described as 'a sort of

Above: Prince Andrew, then aged sixteen, during the school holidays from Gordonstoun. Already he was noted for his dashing good looks.
Below: The Queen Mother on her seventy-fifth birth-

day photographed by Norman Parkinson at Royal Lodge, her home in Windsor Great Park, with her two eldest grandsons, Prince Charles and Prince Andrew.

dormitory rag; a harmless bit of horseplay'. After lights-out, there was a pillow fight in Andrew's dormitory and he fell off a bed and hit his head on the floor. He thought nothing of it, but went to the sick-bay the next morning complaining of a headache. When the real story came out, he was taken to hospital for a check-up, but the X-ray revealed nothing more than a large bump on the head.

During the summer holidays there was a treat for Andrew and his cousins David Linley and Sarah Armstrong-Jones. They were allowed to accompany the Queen and Prince Philip on their tour of the North Sea oil installations, which included the Graythorpe I, a production platform, and the exploration rig Ocean Kokuei. Aboard the Royal Yacht, they visited Aberdeen, the new centre of the exploration fields, and Nigg Bay, where a gigantic £50 million platform was being constructed for use in the Forties Field. From Aberdeen they went on to Balmoral for their traditional summer holiday and the usual round of field sports and family entertainment. Such entertainment always includes Queen Elizabeth the Queen Mother's birthday, if they arrive before 4 August and Princess Anne's birthday on 15 August. Andrew was particularly proud of the presents he had made for his grandmother, a bowl and a vase he had 'thrown' in his pottery class. Like his painting and photography, his pottery showed definite signs of artistic merit.

For the fourteen-year-old Andrew there was another excitement when he was taught to drive, not on the public roads, which would have been illegal, but on the hundreds of miles of estate roads and tracks. When he was a little older, he was given expert driving lessons by Graham Hill, the famous racing driver and World Champion.

Where the Queen, as Princess Elizabeth, and Princess Margaret and the young Charles and Anne had all had French, or French Canadian, tutors or governesses to teach them the language, it was thought better to allow Andrew to join a party of his contemporaries from Gordonstoun on a three-week trip to France. It was an exchange visit of ten boys and five girls with the Caousou Jesuit College near Toulouse in the Languedoc in southwest France. His visit was a masterly well-kept secret, with Scotland Yard liaising with the French police. There was no word in the press, in Britain or in France, until after the three-week visit. Too late was the reporter who saw him on his arrival, only to be told, 'My name is Andrew Edwards. My father is a gentleman farmer and my mother does not work.' His pseudonym came from his first and last Christian names and the reference to his father as a farmer was certainly true, for, as Ranger of Windsor Great Park, he had completely reorganized all the Royal estates and home farms. As to his mother not working, Andrew was indeed far from accurate.

When in Toulouse, Andrew stayed with a doctor and his family in Balma, a fashionable suburb of the city. Outside the school party, only his hosts and the abbot of the Jesuit college knew his real identity. Andrew's French did improve although the lay head of studies, M René Rech, did remark that 'he can hardly be said to speak fluently after only three weeks in France. But he made very considerable progress while he was with us.' Apart from the French and history studies, there was a visit to

Aerospatiale, the French Concorde factory and a football match against the college, which Gordonstoun lost, despite the goal scored by Andrew. The abbot remembered Andrew as 'a lively boy with the good and bad points of any fourteen-year-old'. His French hosts recalled him particularly helpful and polite, while his French studies master in charge of the party declared at the end, 'Mon Dieu he was certainly a handful!'

Andrew launched into his second year at Gordonstoun with enthusiasm. He had earned himself the sobriquet of 'The Sniggerer' from his penchant for telling jokes and bursting into peels of laughter before he had reached the punchline. That Christmas holiday was spent mostly at Sandringham, at Wood Farm House, while the main house was being renovated. There he spent his time with his gun on the estate, walking the hedgerows with his labrador, and accompanying his father and brother on the various Sandringham shoots. Before returning to Gordonstoun, Prince Philip took Andrew on a private visit to stay with some German cousins and to ski. Prince Philip piloted the aircraft himself and the trip was kept a secret.

The Queen and Prince Philip had succeeded in their wish to keep their second son 'private' and out of the public eye. However, as he grew up the press began to take more notice of him. Girls were interviewed by the press. Talking of the discotheque evenings at Gordonstoun, one fourteen-year-old sighed, 'He's a great dancer. I've danced with him many times, but he dances with a lot of girls. Just when you think you are getting somewhere with him he goes off with another girl. I suppose it's for the best really. If he ever got stuck with one girl, she would be eaten alive!' However appealing Andrew was, there was always one major drawback – the detective always came too. One girl close to him complained, 'Andy doesn't seem to notice, but I found it most distracting when we used to go about together. It's a real passion-killer, if you'll excuse the phrase.' Although some of the girls may have been enamoured by a Royal swain, he had his adversaries amongst the boys, possibly through jealousy, as he was particularly successful.

Another aspect of his life that drew attention was the fact that at that time he was second in line to the throne. The more the Prince of Wales, dubbed Action Man, courted danger, either in the air as a trainee helicopter pilot or on the ground in any one of his many chosen sports, the more attention turned to his younger brother. At the age of fifteen, Andrew was suddenly considered as an understudy. In the spring of 1975, there was certainly more than a thought over Andrew's education and possible future role. A Court official was quoted by a Sunday newspaper as saying:

'In this modern age we cannot close our eyes to the fact that Prince Charles could have a fatal accident. He could easily have been killed when a ball grazed his chin when he was playing polo. Twice he has been involved in forced helicopter landings and there were also one or two minor incidents when he was on an Army Commando course. Through no fault of his own when driving his own car, he had three near misses. This is why Prince Andrew, under the direction of his parents and their close advisers, is having a much broader and in

many ways tougher upbringing and education than Prince Charles ever experienced.'

Whether there was any truth in the story or not, the 'understudy' role, conscious or supposed, made little or no difference to Andrew.

The Prince of Wales, by his energy and dogged determination to succeed, has always been 'a hard act to follow'. A traditional method of conquering shyness within the Royal Family is acting. Queen Elizabeth the

Above: Arriving for the Highland Gathering at Braemar, Prince Andrew is wearing the Hunting Stewart tartan and Prince Edward the Balmoral tartan originally designed by Prince Albert, Queen Victoria's husband.
Facing page: The Queen Mother on her birthday in 1976 with four of her grandchildren, (from left to right) Prince Andrew, Viscount Linley, Prince Edward and Lady Sarah Armstrong-Jones.

Queen Mother played a game where she pretended she was some dignitary, such as an Eastern potentate or the Archbishop of Canterbury, and her daughters had to talk to her in her role. Later, they both starred in the 'Windsor Pantomimes' to raise money for Queen Mary's wool fund. Prince Charles followed closely in the Queen's footsteps with his performance of Macbeth, but Andrew could not quite muster a part of that calibre. The Queen and Prince Philip did manage to visit the school to see him perform in a small part in *Simple Spyman,* a farce. Andrew enjoyed his school dramatics although he recognized his limitations. 'I become bored with being myself and like taking on other roles. My brother [Prince Charles] is far better at dramatics. I make a comedian of myself.'

Having seen the installations in the North Sea, Andrew was thrilled and privileged to accompany the Queen to Dyce in the east of Scotland, to witness her pushing the button to start the oil flowing into the refinery at Grangemouth.

Where Andrew did make his mark over his father and brother, and still continues to do so, is in flying. He is a natural and gifted pilot. He began in the Air Training Corps at the Royal Air Force Station at Milltown Airfield, Morayshire, not that far from Gordonstoun. He was fortunate in having one of the most experienced glider instructors, Flight Lieutenant Peter Bullivant. Bullivant found him 'quite fearless and quick to learn' and added that 'he is a very good and enthusiastic young pilot'. He began, at the age of fifteen in November, and was eager to qualify for his wings. Even for a Prince of the Royal blood, Andrew had to wait until he was sixteen before he could fly solo. However, in July the following year, 1976, he made three four-minute circuits of Milltown Airfield and so gained his wings.

Other successes that term were his six 'O' levels, which did not seem to overtax him, and he made it into the cricket First XI. The Royal Family had their excitements and successes too, as Princess Anne was chosen to represent Great Britain in the Three Day Event Team in the Olympic Games to be held at Montreal, Canada. His journey to Canada was to have a far-reaching effect on him, more than he could possibly have imagined when he flew out to join the rest of the Royal Family to witness his sister's perfomance in the Olympic Games.

4

THE CANADIAN EXPERIENCE

Canada, and the Canadians, will always be very special to Andrew and his first visit was for a very special occasion, the XXI Olympic Games held in Montreal in the summer of 1976. The Queen and Prince Philip had completed a highly successful tour of the United States, including a fabulous ball at the White House in Washington as guests of President Ford, then on and up to Montreal to open the Olympic Games. Andrew flew out to join not only them, but his sister and brother-in-law, Princess Anne and Captain Mark Phillips, as well. The selectors had chosen Princess Anne purely on merit and results of past three day events rather than any royal prerogative and it was no mean feat that Mark Phillips was also chosen as reserve with his comparatively inexperienced horses.

For the whole of their trip, the Royal Family stayed aboard the Royal Yacht *Britannia*. The Prince of Wales, then in command of the minehunter HMS *Bronington,* persuaded the Queen to allow Edward, then aged twelve, to join the party. Princess Anne and her husband stayed in the Olympic village, where they lived exactly as the thousands of other competitors. Security for the Royal Family and competitors was necessarily tight, for not only had there been a massacre at the Munich Games in 1972, there was also a particularly active French separatist group. There was, however, no repeat of earlier misfortunes.

Andrew was very much part of the Royal 'team'. He was there for the reception given aboard the Royal Yacht and he was by the Queen's side when she opened the Games. He pointed out his sister, marching in her Olympic uniform, as she entered the stadium.

To all of them, the highlight of the Games was Princess Anne's performance on the Queen's horse Goodwill. They all went to Bromont, where a particularly testing cross-country course had been laid out and they watched from the Royal Box above a packed arena. The crowd responded to the commentator's request for quiet, which Goodwill found unnerving. For that first stage, the dressage test, Goodwill was 'literally bursting with good health'. Twice Goodwill broke out of a trot to a canter, which put her down to twenty-

Princess Anne took part in the 1976 Olympic Games which were opened by the Queen at Montreal in Canada. Photographed here at Bromont the Royal Family came to support Princess Anne.

sixth place after the first day. Most of the spectators left after her performance. That night it rained hard, which made the going heavy on the sand tracks of the cross-country course. The storm that had been gathering behind the hill broke just as Princess Anne started off. The Queen and the rest of the Royal Family were watching at the second fence and were all thrilled to see her going so well. However, at the nineteenth fence her luck ran out. Goodwill slipped on take-off and the Princess hit the ground hard and was concussed. With sheer guts, Princess Anne completed the final seventeen fences. In the show-jumping section, where again the arena was crammed to capacity, the Royal Family watched Princess Anne improve on her overnight position to twenty-fourth.

Andrew's enjoyment of the Olympic Games did not end with the Three Day Event. The sixteen-year-old daughter of a retired Canadian Army colonel, Sandi Jones, was detailed to accompany the tall and attractive Prince for the rest of the Games. At first, she was

Right and below: The Canadian visit during the summer of 1976 was Prince Andrew's first royal tour with his parents. His easy manner and self-confidence made him popular with the crowds. His success prompted the Prime Minister, Pierre Trudeau, to suggest to the Queen and Prince Philip that they send their son to a Canadian college for several terms just as Prince Charles had spent some time at an Australian school.

Gordonstoun, then Lympstone was by far the toughest of them all. There he began his fitness training all over again, he marched over difficult moorland, climbed mountains, spent nights out under canvas on survival training and tackled the formidable assault course. It was a great personal triumph to him to pass out so well and to his father, as Captain General, the Royal Marines were a very special part of the Royal Navy. The then Commandant General of the Royal Marines personally presented Prince Andrew with his coveted green beret with the accolade, 'He is strong, physically fit, but, more important, he has determination.' At last Prince Andrew could see that he had so much to offer in himself without having to resort to his Royal position to impress.

With his intensive training in England and abroad, there was little chance for any 'serious' social life. Prince Andrew had many friends, mostly from his school days or neighbours of the Royal Estates. Much of his 'off-duty' life was spent making up parties with those friends, part of a group rather than with anyone in particular. In general, they were a fun group, ever changing and more of the Tramp set, the more _avant-garde_ nighterie in London's Jermyn Street or Wedgies in the King's Road, rather than Annabels, the more select and exclusive club for the upper strata of society. He was an obvious 'plus' to any society dance or houseparty. One girl, not on the 'debutante' scene, but an obvious candidate for Tramp, with whom Prince Andrew became particularly close, was Carolyn Seaward. A year his junior, she was the daughter of a Devon farmer. She was very pretty and her blonde hair, blue eyes, trim figure and flashing smile earned her the title of Miss United Kingdom. They were much taken with each other and she described him as 'very charming, witty and amusing'. The press hounds were

Above: Midshipman the Prince Andrew during his passing-out parade at the Royal Naval College, Dartmouth in April 1980. The Queen took the salute and inspected the guard of honour.

Below: Prince Andrew wearing the coveted green beret of the Royal Marines at his passing-out parade at the Royal Marine training establishment at Lympstone in Devon.

onto her immediately, but all the Press Office at Buckingham Palace would release was, 'We are not prepared to confirm, deny or comment on such a story.' Prince Andrew simply shrugged off their reports and continued with his life as a young Royal Navy officer.

The 2 April 1980, the day of the passing-out parade at the Royal Naval College at Dartmouth, known as the Lord High Admiral's Divisions, was very special for the Royal Family and the College, for the Queen took the salute and inspected the guard of honour. Mother and son could not help the involuntary smile that flashed between them as Prince Andrew stood to attention, his sword presented before him.

There is no let up in the training of the Royal Navy's helicopter pilots and Prince Andrew was no exception. At the end of April, he was away again on another course, the Aircrew Survival Training at the Royal Naval Safety Equipment School at Seafield Park, near Gosport in Hampshire. There he learned the basic

A lighter moment after the passing-out parade at Dartmouth when Prince Andrew was asked to plant a small sapling beside the larger ones just planted by the Queen and Prince Philip.

Prince Andrew and his brother-in-law, Mark Phillips during a charity clay pigeon shoot near Chester in August 1980. Prince Andrew has been a good shot since his early teens.

skills of first aid, aviation medicine and the use of survival equipment. He had only just passed out of that course before he was off on another, the Elementary Flying Training course at RAF Leeming in Yorkshire. There, the Royal Naval Flying Training Squadron taught their would-be pilots to fly, using the RAF Bulldog aircraft. Prince Andrew, with his previous experience and flying hours clocked up, completed the couse with relative ease, two weeks ahead of the twenty-one week schedule. His instructors realized that in Prince Andrew they had a very natural and gifted pilot. No sooner than he had passed out of RAF Leeming, than he was sent to a management course for junior officers at HMS _Excellent_ at Portsmouth in October, then immediately onto another course on fire-fighting and nuclear, biological and chemical defence. From there in November, he began his training in earnest for his chosen career as a Royal Navy helicopter pilot.

Despite the many and varied courses Prince Andrew attended, there were times of relaxation and leave. He was among the party of Royal cousins for Cowes week aboard the Royal Yacht _Britannia_. It was ostensibly a young party that included, among other non-Royals, Lady Diana Spencer. Following the 'migration', Prince Andrew was at Balmoral, where again Lady Diana Spencer was staying for part of the time, partly to help look after her sister's baby. Lady Jane is married to the Queen's Assistant Secretary, Robert Fellowes. As the world knows, it was during those holidays at Balmoral that news of the friendship between the Prince of Wales and Lady Diana Spencer first made the headlines and started one of the most publicized courtships ever within the Royal Family.

After the summer break of sailing on the Solent and shooting and stalking at Balmoral, Prince Andrew was keen to complete the next stage of his training. In November, he began at the Royal Naval Air Station at Culdrose in Cornwall for further basic flying training on fixed-wing aircraft and, later, to graduate to helicopters. It was a wonderful experience for him, one that he enjoyed enormously. There has been a great tradition within the male members of the Royal Family of flying helicopters and now, Prince Andrew was upholding that tradition and would, in time, extend it. It began with Prince Philip, when he wished to learn. His secretary and friend, Lieutenant Commander Michael Parker, requested permission for him to fly from the then Prime Minister, Winston Churchill. The gruff reply came, 'Is it your intention to wipe out the whole of the Royal Family in the shortest possible time?' There were no such restrictions for Prince Andrew, who was given every possible encouragement from his family and his Service chiefs.

Because he was in the middle of his course, there were no great celebrations on the day of his twenty-first birthday, 19 February 1981. Instead, he drove up to Windsor Castle after his flying instruction for a quiet dinner with the Queen and Prince Philip and other members of the Royal Family. There was great excitement within the family for they all knew of the Prince of Wales's engagement to Lady Diana Spencer. He remained at Windsor and returned, not to Culdrose, but to Buckingham Palace to be there for the excitement of the announcement of the engagement. The day belonged to his brother and fiancée, so he kept out of sight, although he was spied looking out of an upstairs window at the photo-call below in the Palace gardens.

Like the Queen taking the salute at his passing-out parade from Dartmouth, so Prince Andrew had another Royal passing-out parade when he graduated from RNAS Culdrose on 2 April 1981. Not only did he receive his wings as a qualified helicopter pilot, he won the silver salver for passing out top of the course. It was a prize earned solely on merit rather than any Royal nepotism, won by 'his genuine aptitude for helicopter flying and a determination to succeed.' In his uniform of Admiral of the Fleet, the Duke of Edinburgh, himself a seasoned helicopter pilot, proudly presented his son with his 'wings' and the salver. In his speech of congratulation to Prince Andrew and his thirteen colleagues who passed out with him, he reminded them that 'this represents only the end of the beginning. There is a lot more training to be done and a lot more experience to be gained.' Prince Philip knew the form, for Prince Andrew was back not long after for an advanced flying training on the Royal Navy's Sea King helicopters.

Despite this series of courses and training, Prince Andrew did have his leave, family life and share of the general excitement of 'wedding fever' leading up to the great day itself. His twenty-first birthday was marked by a spendid ball at Windsor Castle which was shared with Prince Philip celebrating his sixtieth birthday. It was a magnificent affair, held on the Friday of Royal Ascot Week, 19 June 1981. Over six hundred guests were invited, including Carolyn Seaward, his former girlfriend. He had, in fact, switched twice since Carolyn, first to Gemma Curry, then aged twenty-two and a model, whom he had taken as his partner to the party given for his aunt, Princess Margaret, at London's Ritz Hotel to mark her fiftieth birthday in November the year before. He then took out her cousin, Kim Deas, another very pretty model of the same age.

Soon after the Prince of Wales's engagement was made public, it was announced that Prince Andrew and Prince Edward would act as supporters, supporter being Royal parlance for the best man, at their brother's wedding. Two days before the wedding,

A proud father, Prince Philip is delighted to award Prince Andrew his flying wings when he passed out top of his helicopter flying course at the Royal Naval Air Station at Culdrose in Cornwall.

there was yet another celebration in the Royal Family – the christening of Princess Anne and Captain Mark Phillips's daughter, Zara, born just ten weeks before. They delayed the christening to make absolutely certain that Prince Andrew, a godfather for the first time, would be free.

On the great day of the wedding, Prince Andrew, dressed in his midshipman's uniform, accompanied his brother in the 1902 State Postilion Landau, to St Paul's Cathedral. It was a wonderful day, as the largest ever television audience in the world witnessed that spectacular occasion. Prince Andrew and his younger brother escorted the bridegroom up to the altar steps to wait for the bride's entrance. At the appointed time, he produced the wedding ring, made from a gold nugget found in Wales, then withdrew to his seat. He signed the wedding register simply 'Andrew' – the signature of a Royal Prince.

Once the new bride and bridegroom had set off to Buckingham Palace, Prince Andrew helped his grandmother, Queen Elizabeth the Queen Mother, into their carriage for their own return to the Palace. When the procession had ended, the crowd, in the most ordered

Top: A qualified and experienced helicopter pilot himself, Prince Philip presents Prince Andrew with a silver salver awarded to the top pupil of the course. Above: Prince Andrew has always been close to his sister, Princess Anne and is a frequent visitor to her home, Gatcombe Park in Gloucestershire. Prince Andrew was thrilled to be godparent for the first time to Princess Anne's second child, Zara.

Prince Philip, a member of the British Carriage Driving Team at the Royal Windsor Horse Show in _1981, about to reward his horses with sugar lumps watched by Prince Andrew._

fashion, moved forward to the railings to await the traditional Balcony appearances. Shortly after one o'clock came the first of four appearances. Prince Andrew came out with the rest of the Royal Family, as happy and thrilled as the hundreds of thousands of people around them. At the last appearance, according to lip readers, it was Prince Andrew who whispered to his brother, 'Go on, give her a kiss,' to which the Prince of Wales replied, 'I'm not going in for that caper – there are millions watching.' After a little more persuasion, he turned a blind eye to the 750 million viewers and kissed the new Princess of Wales.

Prince Andrew's part in the wedding was still not over. He had already rescued some helium-filled

Above: Prince Andrew escorts Prince Charles's fiancée, Lady Diana Spencer to Trooping the Colour six weeks before her wedding.
Facing page above: Not noted as an enthusiastic racegoer, Prince Andrew turns out for the traditional carriage drive from Windsor Castle to the Royal Enclosure during the Royal meeting at Ascot. He is seen here accompanying an old friend, the Duchess of Roxburghe.
Facing page below: Despite the heavy schedule of engagements in the weeks before his wedding Prince Charles managed to find time to play polo, occasionally watched by Prince Andrew on leave from the Navy.

balloons from the ball held on the previous Monday in place of a wedding reception and tied them to the carriage that would take the Prince and Princess of Wales away on the first part of their honeymoon. However, thinking them a little tame, he borrowed some lipstick, and he and Edward drew a heart and arrow and wrote JUST MARRIED on a piece of cardboard and tied it to the back of the landau. It was a great success and ably demonstrated just how much it was a family wedding.

The excitement of the wedding died down and Prince Andrew returned to Culdrose to continue his advanced and operational training on Sea King helicopters. On one exercise in the Firth of Clyde, he was engaged in the rescue of a seaman who had fallen overboard. Crew members of the submarine HMS _Ocelot_ were being airlifted from the supply vessel RFA _Engerdine_ in a rough sea and driving rain. Ordinary Seaman John Hendren was swept off the bows of the submarine and into the water. Prince Andrew's helicopter, with him at the controls beside his instructor, was ordered into the rescue. He hovered over the spot where the sailor was swimming while the winchman was lowered to bring the man to safety.

On 1 September 1981, Prince Andrew was finally commissioned to the rank of Sublieutenant, almost two years to the day from when he first arrived at Dartmouth for his basic training. Soon after, on 23 October, he completed his operational training, and four days later he was posted to 820 Squadron on the aircraft carrier HMS _Invincible_. He had lost that brashness of his youth and his self-confidence came solely from what he had achieved himself, rather than relying on who he was. He had also lost that 'little boy' look, his features having hardened through two years of rigorous Royal Navy training. He had also tried to grow a beard. 'A full set of whiskers' is permissible in the Royal Navy and three weeks is the regulation time allowed to grow them. Prince Andrew, to his intense annoyance, was ordered to shave his off by his commanding officer.

Prince Andrew joined one of the largest ships in the Royal Navy. He soon settled into the routine and workings of the ship and her training exercises. Most of all, he relished the fact that at last he had a proper job to do, that he was finally making his own contribution. Others of his family had started much earlier with their official duties, but it was thought that there was no

need to hurry Prince Andrew into the inevitable round of official engagements.

He was, however, asked to speak at the Oxford and Cambridge Centenary Rugby Varsity dinner, his first solo engagement. He endeared himself to them all when he began his speech with a joke about a cannibal father and son who saw an attractive girl in the jungle. 'The son, not well up on the facts of life at all, said: "Look at her, father, why don't we take her home for dinner?" to which the father replied: "I have a better idea, why don't we take her home and eat your mother?"'

Prince Andrew was invited to the wedding of Prince Marie Astrid of Luxembourg to the Archduke of Austria, Christian de Hapsburg-Lorraine, on 7 February 1982. There he met the eighteen-year-old daughter of King Carlos of Spain, Princess Elena. Much was made of their meeting, as a Royal princess was a departure from his usual girlfriends and there was diplomatic friction over Spain's claim to Gibraltar.

The officers and men of HMS _Invincible_ were on exercise in the North Sea when they heard that she was to be sold to the Royal Australian Navy. A deep depression descended over the ship. When interviewed, her captain, Captain Jeremy Black, said the news was 'a great shock'. Prince Andrew would not be drawn to comment, merely to describe his first ship as 'marvellous'. The reprieve for HMS _Invincible_ came from the most extreme circumstances – the outbreak of the war to recover the Falkland Islands from Argentine occupation.

Facing page above: Mrs Nancy Reagan, wife of the American President, joins Prince Andrew in applauding Prince Charles's team, England II successfully beat Spain during a polo match at Smith's Lawn, Windsor a few days before Prince Charles's wedding.
Facing page below: Flanked by an escort of the Household Cavalry, Prince Andrew accompanies his brother on their way to St Paul's Cathedral in the 1902 State Landau for Prince Charles's wedding.
Right: For his first solo public-speaking engagement Prince Andrew addressed the dinner given in honour of the 100th Rugby Varsity Match at the Hilton Hotel in London.

7

TO WAR

HMS *Invincible* sailed for the South Atlantic and to the Falkland Islands on 5 April 1982. She was one of forty ships that made up the initial Task Force. It was a phenomenal piece of organization to mount such an operation in such a short time and at such a great distance. Prince Andrew was just one of the 1,200 complement of officers and crew of HMS *Invincible* and, like every other member of that crew, he played his vital role in the ship, in the air with his helicopter squadron and in the war. Nor would he, his commanding officer or the Royal Family have had it otherwise.

A statement from Buckingham Palace indicated that the Queen was adamant that her son should receive no special treatment as, just before HMS *Invincible* sailed, it was announced that, 'Prince Andrew is a serving officer and there is no question in her mind that he is going.' His commanding officer, the commander of 820 Squadron, Lieutenant Commander Ralph Wykes-Sneyd confirmed that 'I will order Prince Andrew into battle just as I would any of my other pilots. He is a co-pilot and with the others, he gets the same work to do – and he gets no quarter from his fellows. I have found him an extremely capable young man, very competent in the air. He has been with the Squadron a year [seven months on operational duty] and, of course, he is very special to the public – you are conscious of that fact. But he gets no special treatment here, and I am under no instructions from above to treat him any differently from others under my command.'

The crew also treated him as any other young officer. One petty officer confirmed, 'He expects us to treat him like all the others, and there is no side on him at all.' On board HMS *Invincible,* Prince Andrew was simply 'one of the crowd'. He was known affectionately as 'H' – short for HRH or Highness. His easy manner, professional approach and skill at his job had made him part of the team and well liked. His brother officers even included him in their Squadron song book with a parody on, and to the music of, 'Prince Charming' sung by Adam and the Ants. His refrain is:

> 'Don't you ever, Don't you ever
> Stop being Andy showing them you're handsome
> Prince Charming, Prince Charming,
> William Hickey is nothing to be scared of.
> Don't you ever, Don't you ever
> Stop being Randy showing them you're handsome?'

As HMS *Invincible* crossed the equator, Prince Andrew was subjected, willingly, to the sea tradition of the 'crossing the line ceremony'. He had, in fact, crossed the line before when he went on his tour of Africa with his parents for the Commonwealth Conference at Lusaka. For the occasion, he wore a T-shirt with the inscription 'A REAL PRINCE' on the back. King Neptune, who

had come aboard at the equator, accused him of wearing it deliberately and positioning himself in front of the cameras 'so that your mum will see you on television'. The denial of the charge earned him a dousing with red food colorant and a ducking in the jerry-rigged canvas swimming pool rigged on the deck.

The ceremony was a brief relaxation of the stringent routine and a jocular note in the grim task ahead of them. Part of the role of the Sea King helicopter is to ensure the safe passage of the ship. Every minute of the day and night, one of the Squadron is airborn with sonar-equipment trailing in the water listening for enemy submarines. Prince Andrew described it as '98 per cent boredom but, when you have contact, 2 per cent excitement, during which you can hear your own heart beats.' Other duties included the 'milk run' – the ferrying of supplies around the Task Force ships.

Prince Andrew had his first taste of action when the flagship HMS *Hermes* signalled that one of her helicopters had ditched in the sea in the appalling weather conditions. Prince Andrew's helicopter was ordered out to search for survivors. Within minutes he, the co-pilot, was airborne with the pilot Sub-lieutenant Christopher Heweth, the navigator, Lieutenant Ian McAllister, and Leading Aircraftman Arnull, the winchman. The hours of training had finally paid off. The operation was reported in the debriefing as: 'It was a black, cold night and although the sea looked deceptively calm from above, there was a big swell, lightning and rain impairing visibility. We picked up the pilot's distress signal and moved in.

Leading Aircraftman Arnull went down on the winch in the wind and rain. It was his first attempt at such a rescue, although we had practised it often. He was lowered three times before the pilot managed to seize his wrist for long enough in the swell to be dragged into the winch harness. Once Arnull was nearly dragged in the water. The two pilots worked to keep the Sea King into position low over the water for the dangerous minutes, when Arnull told them through the intercom that there could be a crewman trapped inside the still-floating wreckage. But all attempts to find the crewman failed and, although three ships detached themselves from the Task Force to stay behind for a further twenty-four hours in patterned search, he was lost.'

Once they reached the waters of the Falkland Islands, Prince Andrew's helicopter was fully operational. Most of the time they were on action stations, where the whole crew moved about in anti-flash gear of 'white hood, drooping nose and long white gloves'. At best, they flew supplies from ship to ship or to the shore; they also ferried troops to the islands or brought the wounded out. The worst part of their operation was to act as a decoy for the deadly Exocet missile. Prince Andrew explained, 'The helicopter is supposed to hover near the carrier, presenting a large radar target to attract the missile. The idea behind it is that the Exocet comes in low over the waves, and is not supposed to be able to go above 27 feet. So when the missile is coming towards you, you gain height quickly above 27 feet, and it flies harmlessly underneath in theory. But the day HMS *Sheffield* was hit, one Exocet was seen to fly over the mast of the ship, and that is well over 27 feet.' Later, Prince Andrew confided that one of his biggest worries was being hit by one of the Task Force Sea Wolf defence missiles in their search for Argentine aircraft. 'Sea Wolfs locked onto our helicopter three times while we were hovering. It really makes the hair stand up on the back of your neck.'

Throughout the whole campaign, Prince Andrew was in constant danger. He was airborne and witnessed the merchant ship *Atlantic Conveyor* being hit. 'I saw it being struck by the missile and it was something I will never forget. It was horrific. At the same time I saw a 4.5 shell come quite close to us. I saw my ship, *Invincible,* fire her missiles. Normally I would say it was spectacular, but it was my most frightening moment of the war.' Another frightening time was when HMS *Sheffield* was hit. He admitted that, 'one really did not know which way to turn and what to do. I did not know where I was and I was fairly frightened then.' Another worry was the effect that the Argentine false reports might have on his family.

Prince Andrew played his part in the rescue of twenty-five of the crew of the *Atlantic Conveyor* from a life raft. They had been buffeted around in the heavy sea for about an hour and a half, when the Sea King helicopter, co-piloted by Prince Andrew, appeared. One of the survivors described the scene. 'The weather was dreadful. It was very cold and the waves were about 20 feet high. We were like sardines in our life raft, one on top of the other. Prince Andrew was very cool, just like the rest of the helicopter crew. He and the rest of the helicopter crew did a great job.'

There were lonely moments, too, for Prince Andrew, 'when you are in your anti-flash protective head and arm clothing and someone has told you to hit the deck because we are under attack. There is nothing worse than this happening when you are in a ship. You have to wait and lie there and only wait and hope.'

In the final push forward to the capture of Port Stanley and after, Prince Andrew also played his part, alongside the thousands of other servicemen. After the surrender of the garrison of Port Stanley, he was still operational, ferrying weapons and supplies to the troops. Although the work load was just as heavy, the actual danger had gone. At the end of the hostilities there was a chance to telephone home from the Royal Fleet Auxiliary *Sir Bedivere* anchored in Port Stanley Harbour. Exactly like every other member of the Task Force, he queued to make his call to the Queen at Buckingham Palace. 'I made the call and she was in. It is about the right time of the evening. She was quite surprised to hear my voice. Her first words to me were that she wanted to say how proud she was of the armed forces, particularly on the ships and for me to pass the message that it had been a marvellous operation.' Another link from home was the delivery of

Top: A serving officer in 802 Squadron in the Falklands Islands campaign, Prince Andrew gives an interview to a London Fleet Street reporter in Port Stanley after the town had been recaptured from the Argentinians.

Above: To his fellow officers on board HMS Invincible, *Prince Andrew was known simply as 'H', short for His Royal Highness.*

post, often held up through the fighting, as was his home. Prince Andrew had his share, besides those from girlfriends, from all members of his family. Late on 21 June, he returned to the Ward Room to a barrage of good-natured ribaldry and his brother officers told him of the birth of Prince William and how he had slipped down a place in the order of succession.

Prince Andrew had a chance to visit the capital, Port Stanley. He had not lost his humour either, describing it as 'rather a nice little town, but a bit muddier than I expected. The perfect place to bring my bride on my honeymoon!' To the delight of the locals, he toured the town on foot and in a captured Argentine jeep with his commanding officer, Lieutenant Commander Ralph Wykes-Sneyd and Lieutenant Commander Nigel Ward, commander of 801 Harrier Squadron. He visited Government House, where he met the Commander of the British Land Forces, Major General Jeremy Moore and other senior officers. For the very first time he was accorded a privilege that was not altogether commensurate with his Royal Naval rank, but one that he had certainly earned. Throughout the campaign, Prince Andrew had fought as was expected of him in the traditions of the Royal Navy and of his family. As he told the _Daily Telegraph_ correspondent, 'It simply never occurred to me that, because I'm a member of the Royal Family, I wouldn't take part if it came to fighting or seeing it through. I was jolly glad that I was here throughout with my squadron: they are absolutely fantastic.' He continued, 'The spirit has been there all the time, and the support has been there from the people who have really showed so much support and faith in what we have done out here and what we are doing. It is absolutely amazing.'

Two months after the cessation of hostilities HMS _Invincible_ was sent home to England. She returned to a tumultuous welcome befitting the victorious Task Force, the ships that included HMS _Invincible,_ and her crew that included Prince Andrew.

Shortly after his return from the Falkland Islands, Prince Andrew returned to flying duties at RNAS Culdrose in Cornwall.

8

THE FUTURE

Throughout his life, Prince Andrew has been compared to his brother, the Prince of Wales. After the return of the Task Force, Prince Charles did admit that he was envious of his younger brother in that he had 'tested' himself in battle conditions, something which he had never done and was never likely to do either. He believes that 'it is terribly important to see how you react and to be tested'. For the first time, Prince Andrew had the edge on his elder brother.

At a press conference after she docked at Portsmouth, the captain of HMS *Invincible*, Captain Jeremy Black, said of the Falkland Islands Campaign: 'I think we have all come back to some extent very changed people ... the young in particular have benefited from what they went through.' Although he was speaking of every member of his ship's complement, his remarks applied to Prince Andrew just as much as to the other twelve hundred officers and men. Sublieutenant Prince Andrew exemplified the very best of those brave men of the Task Force; the fact that he was a member of the popular Royal Family, and good looking as well, only endeared him further to the nation.

It was an experience that none of them wished to forget. Prince Andrew donated his signed kid-leather gloves that he had worn throughout the campaign to be auctioned, the proceeds of £500 going to the Falklands Appeal and the South Atlantic Fund to aid those, civilians as well as Servicemen, who had suffered in the war. It was Prince Andrew's wish that he should, and did, lay a wreath to commemorate his colleagues who had died in the campaign at the Cenotaph at the annual Remembrance Day parade which took place on 14 November 1982.

After the longest tour ever by an aircraft carrier, 166 days at sea, Prince Andrew, like most of the ship's company, was given shore leave. A special welcome had been arranged for him at Balmoral. The estate workers had decorated a rowing-boat, and, to the skirl of bagpipes, he was hauled in it through the gates, in the rain, to the Castle. It was a happy homecoming for the whole family.

His part in the Falklands' Campaign had successfully squashed his reputation as a mere Royal 'playboy'. Although the tabloid press were quick to point out any

---

Wearing his Falklands' Campaign Medal and Silver Jubilee Medal, Prince Andrew arrives with other members of the Royal Family for the Service of Remembrance at the Royal Albert Hall in London.

The flying gloves worn by Prince Andrew during the Falkland Islands Campaign. They were later auctioned at his request in aid of the South Atlantic Fund and Falklands Appeal and raised £500.

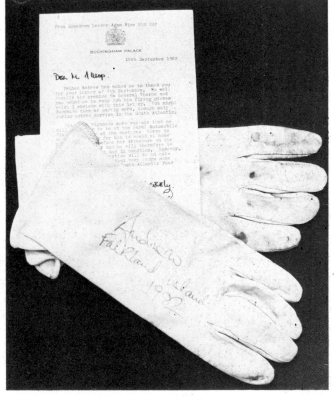

supposed new girlfriend in his life to make a good story, they were generally inaccurate in their reporting as Prince Andrew was careful 'to cover his tracks'. However, he was unlucky to be spotted by a *Daily Express* photographer on a scheduled British Airways flight to Barbados. He was with his girlfriend, Kathleen, better known as Koo, Stark, travelling as Mr and Mrs Cambridge and three other friends. Prince Andrew had been introduced to Koo at Tramps by the impresario Michael White in February and they had corresponded all the time he was in the South Atlantic. She had also been to stay for three days at Balmoral, as part of a large house-party. She was twenty-five, dark and pretty, but her previous claim to fame was her part in two erotic films when she was aged seventeen.

'Mr and Mrs Cambridge and their party' were bound for the Caribbean island of Mustique to stay in his aunt's, Princess Margaret's, house, *Les Jolies Eaux.* As they boarded a private aircraft, it was obvious to all that they were bound for Mustique, eighty miles to the south-west of Barbados, and the world's press descended on the tiny island. Princess Margaret's three-bedroomed house is set on a promontory to the south of the island with spectacular views over the southern Grenadines, a chain of islands which form part of St Vincent. The garden, originally planned by Roddy Llewelyn, slopes away from the house and is well screened by scrub and a pair of gatehouses. There is a swimming pool, a palm-covered gazebo and steps down to a spectacular white beach, Gelliceau Bay. Mustique, the 'smartest unsmart holiday island' has a reputation for being discreet and is remote enough to be 'safe' from all but the most determined. But Prince Andrew was not to be allowed to enjoy the delights of Mustique and his party. Although Koo's mother was also staying in the house, endless stories and photographs filtered back through the media.

Stories, mostly apochryphal, appeared on the front pages of all the world's press and clips of Koo's films were screened on national television news bulletins. After a week of being besieged in the house, Prince Andrew finally gave up the unequal struggle and flew back to England with his detective, from Antigua under the name of Mr Newham. To make matters worse, one of his party, American journalist Elizabeth Solomon, was approached for her story of the holiday, but although it was never published, the implication that there was something seriously amiss was there. Prince Edward, on a sabbatical teaching post after Gordonstoun in New Zealand, summed up the general feeling, 'He was only a sailor. He'd been at war; he wanted to get away from everything and relax, unwind and get some sun. He'd missed summer, and he'd every right to go on holiday. Not only did they [the press] hound him over the affair, they actually hounded him to such an extent that he had to stop the holiday. He came back from that holiday more drawn, more tired than he had from three months at war, and I think to treat someone who's just come back from serving their country like that is absolutely despicable.'

Like all 'flash' stories, his sojourn in Mustique with Koo soon died after his return to duty with his Squadron, again based at Culdrose in Cornwall. The press besieged the base, but Prince Andrew was shielded by his brother officers and they soon lost interest. One lesson that he did learn from the whole affair was that, in future, he had to be far more circumspect where his love life was concerned. The lesson learned, they were able to meet in the homes of trusted friends.For instance, Prince Andrew was able to take her to Floors Castle, the home of the Duke and Duchess of Roxburghe in Scotland.

Now following in the wake of the Princess of Wales, Prince Andrew undertook his second public engagement – the switching on of the Christmas illuminations on Regent Street in London. He was an outstanding success with unprecedented crowds straining to see him. In his speech, he made a reference to the Christmas tree, 'Some people attribute their introduction to my great-great-great-grandfather [Prince Albert, Queen Victoria's Consort]. They were regarded as a pagan and a continental attempt to supplant the traditional yule log. However, the tree has become so much part of the British Christmas that we think we have invented it ourselves.'

The traditional Royal Christmas was spent at Windsor Castle with the equally traditional New Year spent at Sandringham. His leave was soon over, and at the end of January he returned to his Squadron, this time back to HMS *Invincible,* who had just completed her sea trials after a refit. His ship sailed from Portsmouth on a NATO exercise, then went on a goodwill mission to the United States of America, the coast of Florida being the first port of call. Again the press made much of the fact that Koo Stark had taken a house nearby with her mother for the period that spanned Prince Andrew's visit and his twenty-third birthday.

In London, there were unprecedented moves by the Press Office at Buckingham Palace to prevent the

Facing page: Prince Andrew's girlfriend, Miss Koo Stark whom he took on holiday to the Caribbean Island of Mustique after his return from the Falkland Islands Campaign.

Above: Prince Andrew at the Cenotaph having just laid a wreath at the Remembrance Day parade to commemmorate those who had died during the Falklands Campaign.

Above: Following in the steps of his sister-in-law, the Princess of Wales, Prince Andrew turns on the Christmas lights in Regent Street, one of London's smartest shopping streets.

Left: When HMS Invincible *visited Barbados, Prince Andrew enjoyed his shore leave in the company of pretty girls.*

Facing page above: Wearing his flying overalls, Prince Andrew with two lieutenants sunbathing on the flight deck of HMS Invincible.

Facing page below: Prince Andrew (facing the camera) after morning Divisions on HMS Invincible. *The officers are wearing their tropical whites called 5 W's which are worn between the Tropics and in 'warm waters' during the summer.*

publication of a series of articles dictated by a former storeman employed by the Palace. Much of the material contained references to Prince Andrew and Koo Stark but the injunction from the High Court stopped all but one of the stories appearing.

The 'lovelife' of a prince of Royal blood to the press is much more exciting than the log of one of Her Majesty's ships. The inevitable reports filtered back of pretty girls in the Bahamas who had been escorted by Prince Andrew, some more, with accompanying photographs, with a party in Barbados and again in

Gibraltar. There however, the presence of Prince Andrew was played down due to the volatile situation between Britain and Spain over the sovereignty of the Rock of Gibraltar.

For the foreseeable future, Prince Andrew will continue in his present role as a helicopter pilot in the Royal Navy. He will be promoted steadily throughout his twelve-year commission, and most likely renew it for a further period to take him through the 1990's. It is virtually certain that the Queen will confer on him a Royal Dukedom. The precedents are, after all, there. Since 1337, the younger sons of the Sovereign who have reached adulthood have been made dukes, although history has proved some of them to have been 'unlucky'. Also, Royal Dukedoms, except for Cornwall (the Prince of Wales) and Lancaster (the Queen) are only titles and do not carry any inherited lands and estates. The most likely title for Prince Andrew is the Duke of York, like the two previous holders of that title and both second sons – his grandfather, George VI, and his great-grandfather, George V. Both acceded to the throne through the respective ab-

dication and death of their older brothers. With Prince Andrew as third in line to the throne, after the Prince of Wales and Prince William of Wales, his chances of emulating the two previous Dukes of York by succeeding to the throne are slim, particularly as it is likely that the Prince and Princess of Wales will have many more children who will then take precedence over him, whether boy or girl.

Instead, Prince Andrew's role will, in a sense, be just as important. Where the Sovereign, by definition, has to remain above the people, Prince Andrew has ably shown that he has 'the common touch' and can successfully link the two estates. With his drive, determination and proven direction in life, his successful future is assured.

Prince Andrew piloted himself to the Biggin Hill Air Show in Kent in a Wessex helicopter of the Queen's Flight. Moving up in his career as a helicopter pilot in the Royal Navy, Prince Andrew has left 820 Squadron and its Sea Kings to train as a Lynx pilot.